AMAZING COIN TRICKS

Written by
Kirk Charles

Illustrated by
Viki Woodworth

Library of Congress Catalog-in-Publication Data
Charles, Kirk.
Amazing coin tricks / by Kirk Charles; illustrated by Viki Woodworth.
p. cm.
Summary: Provides instructions for a variety of coin tricks.
ISBN 1-56766-084-3
1. Coin tricks—Juvenile literature.
[1. Coin tricks. 2. Magic tricks.]
I. Woodworth, Viki, ill.   II. Title
GV1559.C43 1995   93-29259
793.8–dc20   CIP/AC

For magic tricks to be wonderful and mysterious, there are certain rules you must follow:

1. Never reveal the secrets of the magic! Doing so ruins the magic and spoils the fun.

2. Never tell the audience what you are going to do before you do it. Surprise is very important to making good magic.

3. Never repeat the trick for the same audience during the same show. They will know what's going to happen and will probably figure out how it's done.

4. Stories make the magic more mysterious. So make up a story that will go with each trick.

5. Practice each trick many times before you show it to anyone. Without practicing, you might accidentally reveal the secret.

Here's a riddle for you.
How many heads are on a quarter?
Two! President Washington's head is
on one side, and the eagle's head is
on the other.

Everybody's Dream

If you could really do magic, wouldn't you pull money out of the air? Here's a way to do just that.

What happens: You reach into the air and make a coin appear.

What you need: A special coin.

Before the show begins, take a small piece of cellophane tape and make a loop. Stick the loop of tape on a quarter. You should be wearing pants. Now stick the special coin to the back of your right thigh, near your back pocket. People standing in front of you shouldn't be able to see the coin.

1. Tell your audience you're going to do something amazing. Look up and pretend to see something.

2. Show that both your hands are empty, and then reach into the air with your left hand.

3. At the same time, drop your right hand to your right side and peel the coin off your leg.

4. Pretend to catch something with your left hand, and then pretend to place what you caught into your right hand. Bring both hands together, making sure no one sees the coin in your right hand yet.

5. Separate your hands and show the coin in your right hand.

Everybody's Dream Part II

Magic money has a mysterious way of vanishing too quickly!

    What happens: The quarter disappears and then comes back.

    What you need: The special coin from the last trick.

1. Stick the special coin to your right hand, in the center of your palm. Show the coin in your right hand.

2. Show your left hand empty and then turn it palm up.

3. Move your right hand, with the coin in it, until it is just above your left hand. Make sure that your right fingers point to the left and your left fingers point straight ahead. (See illustration.)

4. Turn your right hand over. People will think the coin is falling into your left palm, but it can't fall, because of the tape.

5. Curl your left fingers around the back of your right hand.

6. Bring out your right hand. Keep your right hand palm down, flat, and open your fingers.

7. As your right hand leaves your left hand, close your left fingers. People will think the coin is in your left hand.

8. Drop your right hand to your right side.

9. Look at your left hand and then slowly open the fingers, showing that the coin has disappeared.

10. At the same time, use your right fingers to pull the coin off the tape in your right palm.

11. As soon as you have shown the audience your left hand, reach into the air with your right hand and pretend to catch the coin. Show the coin and drop it into your left hand.

R looks as if coin falls into left hand but is stuck to right

Brush-Off

This isn't a trick – it's more of a challenge to your friends.

    What happens: You ask your friends to brush a quarter out of your hands. They can't.

    What you need: A quarter and a hairbrush.

1. Place the coin into the center of your palm.

2. Hand your friend a brush and ask her to brush the coin off your hand. (Illustration.)

3. As long as she brushes in a normal way, the coin will stay in your hand. She can brush front to back or back to front – or even side to side – and the coin will stay.

Keep coin in center of palm

Six Cents for Your Thoughts

Would you like to read minds – or at least look as though you can? Well, here's a way to do that.

What happens: Without looking, you tell your friend which of her hands has a penny and which has a nickel.

What you need: A friend who can multiply and add two-digit numbers in her head.

1. Hand your friend a nickel and a penny.

2. Ask her to put the coins behind her back and mix them up, so you won't know which coin is in which hand. Turn away so you can't see what she is doing.

3. Once she has finished mixing the coins and has one in each hand, ask her to extend her closed hands toward you. (Illustration.)

4. Ask her to multiply the coin in her right hand by 14. Watch how fast she does it.

5. Now ask her to multiply the coin in her left hand by 14. Watch how fast she does it. The hand that takes the longest to multiply has the nickel.

The hand that is the quickest has the penny. It's much easier to multiply something by one than by five!

6. Now ask her to add up the two numbers and tell you the sum. The sum doesn't matter, but it helps to disguise what you are really doing.

7. Repeat the number. Then say, "That means the nickel is in this hand and the penny is in the other hand." Point to the correct hands.

8. If you want to repeat the trick, use a different number like 12, 13, 15, or 16. Don't use 10 or 11 – it's too easy.

← watch to see which hand takes longer to multiply

Coin Catching

This is more of a stunt than a trick. It's great for show-offs!

    What happens: You balance a coin on your elbow, toss it into the air, and catch it.

    What you need: A quarter and time to practice.

1. Raise your left arm, with your hand palm down. Now bend your left arm at the elbow, so that your palm turns face up. Your left fingers should be near your ears. (See illustration.)

2. Place a quarter near your elbow.

3. Now quickly bring down your left hand to straighten your arm and catch the coin as it leaves your elbow. It helps if you bend your knees as you make the toss.

With practice, you can stack several quarters on top of each other and catch them!

← with practice you can do several coins

All Wet

You've heard of mad money? This is sad money
– so sad, it cries!

    What happens: You squeeze a coin and it cries.

    What you need: A quarter and a small piece of
wet cotton or small wet sponge.

1. Hide the small sponge behind the coin.

2. Explain that you're going to squeeze the coin and make it cry.

3. When you squeeze, you're really squeezing the sponge behind the coin so that the water drips out of it. (Illustration.)

hold wet
cotton ball
behind coin

On Edge

This is another challenge for your friends.

What happens: Ask your friend to balance a quarter on the edge of a dollar bill. He can't do it, so you show him how.

What you need: A quarter and a fairly new dollar bill.

1. Ask your friend to balance a quarter on the edge of a dollar bill. He tries but can't do it.

2. Offer to show him how. Fold the dollar bill in half lengthwise and then again widthwise. Be sure the folds are sharp.

3. Put the bill on a table, with the creased part up.

4. Balance the quarter on the fold. (See illustration.)

5. Slowly straighten the bill. As you do, lift it off the table. The quarter should remained balanced on the edge.

carefully pull
folded dollar open

Oops!

Instead of using sleight of hand, you're going to use sleight of foot!

    What happens: You make a coin disappear.

    What you need: A coin.

1. Hold a coin in your right hand.

2. Drop the coin near your left foot. Pretend that dropping it is accidental. (Make sure you're wearing shoes.)

3. Move your foot very close to the coin.

4. As you bend down to pick up the coin, flick it under your shoe. (Illustration.)

5. Pretend to pick up the coin, and then pretend to put it in your other hand.

6. Say a magic word and show that both your hands are empty – the coin has disappeared.

7. Walk away from the coin, *without* looking at it.

8. Pretend to see the coin in the air. Then pretend to watch it fall and land on the floor.

9. Point at the coin, then pick it up.

← slide coin
under foot

Eagle Under Glass

This trick works best when you perform it for only one or two people.

What happens: You trap a quarter underneath a glass of water and it seems to become invisible.

What you need: A quarter and a clear glass, half full of water.

1. Place the quarter on your left palm.

2. Place the glass of water on top of the quarter.

3. Ask your friends if they can see the coin. They'll say they can.

4. Put your right hand on top of the glass. (See illustration.)

5. Now ask if they can see the coin. They won't be able to.

6. Tell them you've made it invisible. Then say you'll bring it back.

7. Remove your right hand, then remove the glass. The coin is in your left hand.

keep coin in center of palm

Presto Changeo

For your big finale, you'll change some change.

What happens: You make a quarter change into a dime.

What you need: Lots of loose coins, including at least a dime, a quarter, and a half dollar. If you don't have a half dollar, a foreign coin as big as a half dollar will work just as well.

1. Put the loose change into your left hand.

2. Remove the half dollar and put it on the table.

3. As you move the coins around in your hand, place a quarter on top of a dime. Make sure they're near the center of your palm.

4. Remove all the other coins and place them in your pocket or purse.

5. Show the quarter in your hand, making sure the dime doesn't show.

6. Show the half dollar and place it on top of the quarter.

7. Keep your left hand palm up, but loosely close your fingers.

8. Reach into your closed left hand and remove the half dollar together with the quarter hidden underneath it. People will think you're taking just one coin, but you're really taking two. (Illustration.)

9. Put the half dollar and the hidden quarter away.

10. Ask what is left in your hand. People will say the quarter.

11. Say a magic word, open your hand, and show the dime.

remove
quarter that
was hidden
under half-dollar

→

←hide dime
under quarter

This Book Is About Magic Tricks Using Coins.

It is written by a real magician, Kirk Charles. Kirk has performed thousands of magic shows, some for children and some for grown-ups. He has done magic for television shows, commercials, and movies. He has also written magic books for magicians.

Kirk wants you to know that he did not invent these tricks. They came from many different sources. Kirk learned some from books and some from other magicians.

The way to learn the tricks is to do them! So make sure you have all the items you need as you read the tricks.

Kirk hopes that you will learn some of these tricks and practice them before you do them. People of all ages love good magic, and the way to perform good magic is to practice!

Read all the instructions for each trick before trying it. If you read something you don't understand, ask your mom, your dad, your older brother, or your older sister to help. But ask them to keep the trick secret.